ENDORSEMENTS FOR THE JESUS MOMENTS SERIES

"Jesus is always far better and far more interesting than we think he is, and seeing how the Old Testament points to him is a great way to find out how. These wonderful books will help us see more and more of Jesus."

SAM ALLBERRY, Associate Pastor at Immanuel Church, Nashville; Author of *Why Bother with Church?* and *James For You*

"When we teach children that the stories from the Old Testament culminate in Christ, they begin to understand that he is the center of the Bible's story. This series highlights Jesus, the hero of every Bible story, and encourages readers to keep him at the center of their stories too."

HUNTER BELESS, Founder and Host of the Journeywomen podcast; Author of *Read It, See It, Say It, Sing It*

"I smiled from ear to ear. My daughters came alive when they caught on. Hidden in this engaging true story is another *even more exciting*. We flipped backward and forward, all the while learning the biblical story and freshly encountering Christ."

DAVID MATHIS, Senior Teacher and Executive Editor at desiringGod.org; Pastor of Cities Church, Saint Paul; Author of *Rich Wounds*

"We want our kids to see that the Old Testament points to Christ. In her marvelous *Jesus Moments* series, Alison Mitchell helps children seek-and-find the Old Testament connection to Jesus in fun ways they'll be sure to remember!"

DANIKA COOLEY, Author of *Bible Investigators: Creation; Bible Road Trip*™ and *Help Your Kids Learn and Love the Bible*

"Alison Mitchell draws children into a rich, true way of reading the Old Testament. The books are fresh, lively, attractive, intriguing and thought-provoking. Warmly recommended."

CHRISTOPHER ASH, Author and Writer-in-Residence at Tyndale House, Cambridge

"This *Jesus Moments* series is a delight! The clear and plain teaching of God's word, coupled with the intriguing illustrations and cleverly hidden symbols, make these books a win-win!"

MARY K. MOHLER, President's wife at SBTS in Louisville, Kentucky; Founder and Director of Seminary Wives Institute; Author of *Growing in Gratitude*

"What a clever series! By using symbols that children must find and explore, these books draw out significant links between Old Testament characters and Jesus. Perfect for parents and teachers who want to help their children understand God's big story."

BOB HARTMAN, Author of *The Prisoners, the Earthquake, and the Midnight Song* and YouVersion's *Bible App for Kids*

Jesus Moments: Moses
© The Good Book Company 2024

Illustrated by Noah Warnes | Design & Art Direction by André Parker | All rights asserted

"The Good Book For Children" is an imprint of The Good Book Company Ltd
North America: thegoodbook.com UK: thegoodbook.co.uk Australia: thegoodbook.com.au
New Zealand: thegoodbook.co.nz India: thegoodbook.co.in

ISBN: 9781784989828 | JOB-007467 | Printed in India

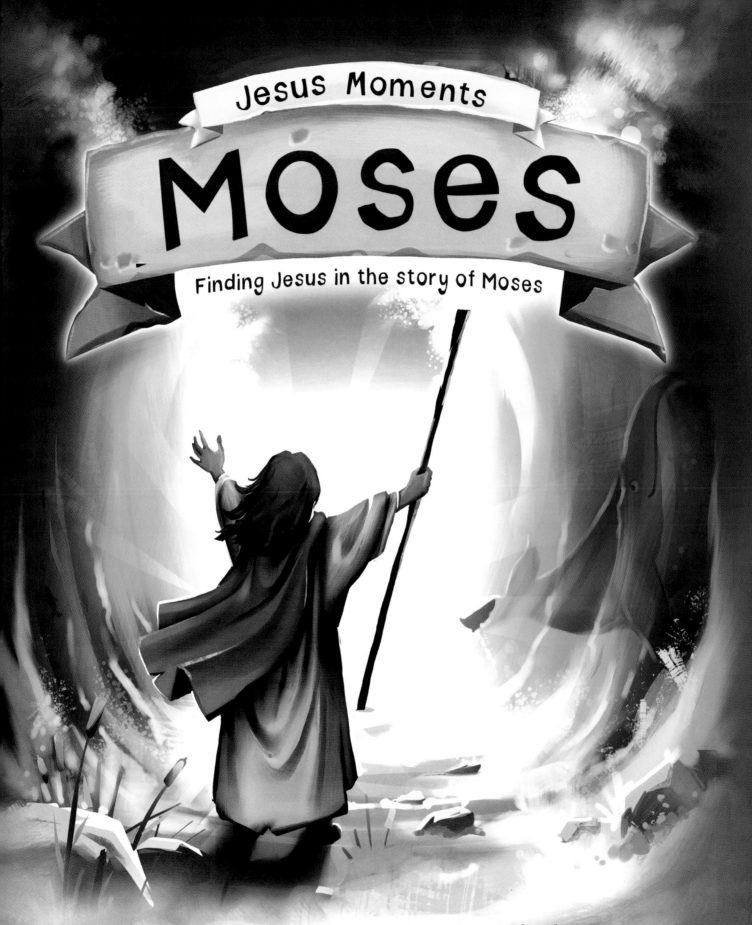

Jesus Moments

Moses

Finding Jesus in the story of Moses

Written by **Alison Mitchell**   Illustrated by **Noah Warnes**

Did you know that the oldest stories in the Bible are a bit like puzzles? If you look carefully, you can spot some

"Jesus moments".

These are moments when someone or something in the story is a little bit like **Jesus**.

So this book is the exciting true story of how God used **Moses** to rescue his people. But what makes it even more exciting is that it's also about **Jesus**, the greatest Rescuer of all.

As you read about **Moses**, keep a lookout for some hidden **bulrushes**. Each time you spot one, that's a clue that there's a **Jesus moment** to find as well.

So let's get started...

Crash! Roar! Splash!

Just as the sun came up and the last person had
stepped onto dry land, the huge walls of water
poured over the path on which the people had
crossed the sea.

God's people had been slaves in Egypt. But God rescued them, and then he made a **huge wind** blow across the Red Sea to give them a dry path so they could cross it. Now his people were safe on the other side — and their enemies were no more.

But that wasn't the end of the journey for the Israelites. God had **much more** to teach them.

After three days in the desert, the people found water. But it was too bitter to drink. **"What are we to drink?"** they grumbled.

So God showed Moses a piece of wood to throw into the water. At once the water became sweet and delicious. God had **saved** them once more.

But instead of them being grateful, soon the grumbling began again. "I'm hungry!" "There's nothing to eat." "We had all the food we wanted in Egypt. But now we're going to starve!"

Grumble, grumble, grumble...

So God said to Moses, "I will make food rain down from the sky. Tell the people that I will send them meat in the evening and bread in the morning."

Moses told the people that God would give them the food they needed. And he did!

The morning food looked like flakes of frost on the ground. "What is it?" the people asked. So they called it **manna**, which means "What is it?" in their language.

A while later they came to a big mountain, called
Mount Sinai. The people camped at the bottom while
Moses went up to the top.

God gave Moses some rules to live by so that the
Israelites would know how to live as God's people.
The most famous are called the
Ten Commandments.

While Moses was on the mountain, the people started to grumble again. "What has happened to Moses? We don't know where he is." And then they did something terrible.

Instead of trusting **God**, who had saved them so many times, they asked Moses' brother, Aaron, to make them a new "god". So Aaron made them a **golden statue** of a calf. But it wasn't really a god. It was just a statue.

The next day the Israelites had a huge party. They sang.
They danced. And they prayed to the statue they had made.

"Thank you for saving us," they said, as if the statue was the
real God. **But it wasn't!**

God was very angry. "Go back down the mountain," he said to
Moses. "The people have turned away from me. So now I will
turn away from them."

But Moses pleaded for the people. "Please don't kill them. Remember the **promises** you have made – that these will be your people. Please forgive them." So God was merciful and forgave his people.

You might think that, after that, the Israelites would love and obey God. But they didn't. No, they turned away from him again and again. The Bible calls this **sin**.

Moses went up and down the mountain
several times to speak with God. While he
was with God, his face began to **glow.**

His face shone so **brightly** that the people were afraid to look at him! So Moses put a veil over his face whenever he had been talking with God.

But still the people kept grumbling. They even complained about the manna God gave them each morning. So God sent poisonous snakes into the camp. Anyone bitten by a snake died.

"Help us!" the people said to Moses. "We were wrong to grumble. Please pray that God will take the snakes away."

So Moses did pray – and God told him what to do.

"Make a snake out of bronze and put it up on a pole. If anyone who is bitten looks up at that snake, they will live."

And that's exactly what happened. God had **saved** his people.

Moses led the Israelites for 40 years. All through that time, God cared for his people, and he saved them again and again.

What a **wonderful rescuing God!**

Now it's time to spot some **Jesus moments.**

Look back at the pictures in the book. Did you spot the special bulrushes? They appear every time there is a Jesus moment in the story.

Each Jesus moment is a moment when something in the story of Moses is a little like Jesus, the Son of God. Did you find all four? Here's what they mean...

When God's people were in the desert, there was no food for them. So Moses told the people that God would **provide** the food they needed. Then God sent them manna every morning.

When a crowd of people followed Jesus up a hill, there was no food for them either. But Jesus was God and could **provide** what the people needed. So Jesus took one boy's packed lunch and used it to feed thousands of people!

When Moses went up Mount Sinai, God gave him the **Ten Commandments**, and many other commands, so that the Israelites would know how to live as God's people.

When Jesus was asked which of **God's commands** was the greatest, he said they could be summed up like this: "Love God with all your heart and soul and mind and strength; and love your neighbour as you love yourself."

When Moses spent time with God, his face **shone** brightly.
It showed that he had **been with God.**

When Jesus took three of his friends up a mountain, Jesus' face and body **shone** brightly too. It showed that **Jesus IS God!**

God sent snakes into the Israelite camp to punish the people for their sin. But God was so kind that he made a way for the people to be forgiven. When the people looked up at the bronze snake on a **pole**, they were saved from the snake bite. They didn't die and could enjoy living as part of God's people.

Death is still the punishment for sin. But God is so kind that he made the only way to be forgiven — for us too. Just as the bronze snake was put up on a pole, so Jesus was put up on a **cross** to die. And when we trust in Jesus, we can be forgiven for our sin too and can enjoy living with God and his people for ever.

God is the great **rescuing** God. He saved
his people at the time of Moses.

God is the great **giving** God. He provided
everything his people needed.

And he still saves his people and gives us
everything we need today through Jesus.

So let's not be grumblers like the Israelites!
Instead, let's be grateful to our **Rescuing
and Giving God.**

Why look for "Jesus Moments"?

The oldest parts of the Bible were written hundreds or even thousands of years before Jesus was born, and yet they all point to him! And when we read the accounts of many Old Testament characters, we can see moments when they are a little bit like Jesus himself.

These "Jesus moments" help us to see Old Testament stories afresh and to understand more deeply who Jesus is and why he came.

The Old Testament story of Moses starts with him being rescued as a tiny baby left in the bulrushes (Exodus 2 v 1-10), follows his life as leader of the Israelites, and ends with God showing him a glimpse of the promised land (Deuteronomy 34 v 1-12). We have only touched on a few parts of his life in this storybook. If you read the full Bible account, you will spot other "moments" when something in the life of Moses pointed towards the life of Jesus Christ, the Son of God.

It was always God's good plan to send his Son to live on Earth, to die for our sins and then to rise to life again. And God gave his people lots of clues about how this would happen.

The risen Jesus told his followers that the Old Testament Scriptures are about him: "And beginning with Moses and all the Prophets, he explained to them what was said in all the Scriptures concerning himself" (Luke 24 v 27). So when we read exciting Old Testament stories, we can look out for those same clues – those "Jesus moments" that point to the even more exciting story of Jesus himself.